D1378532

ENERGY

Finding New Grace for the Pace

By Beth Jones

Harrison House
Tulsa, OK

All Scripture quotations are taken from *The King James Bible*, unless otherwise noted.

Scripture quotations marked (AMP) are taken from the *Amplified Bible*, Copyright © 1954, 1958, 1962, 1964, 1965, 1987 by the Lockman Foundation. Used by permission.

Scripture quotations marked (NLT) are taken from the Holy Bible, *New Living Translation*, Copyright © 1996. Used by permission of Tyndale House Publishers, Inc., Wheaton, Illinois 60189. All rights reserved.

Scripture quotations marked (NKJV) are taken from the *New King James Version*. Copyright © 1982 by Thomas Nelson, Inc. Used by permission. All rights reserved.

Scripture quotations marked (NIV) are taken from the *HOLY BIBLE, NEW INTERNATIONAL VERSION®, NIV®*. Copyright © 1973, 1978, 1984 by International Bible Society. Used by permission of Zondervan. All rights reserved.

The Message: Scripture quotations marked (The Message) are taken from *The Message* by Eugene H. Peterson, Copyright © 1993, 1994, 1995, 1996, 2000, 2001, 2002. Used by permission of NavPress Publishing Group. All rights reserved.

Scripture quotations marked (TLB) are taken from *The Living Bible*, Copyright © 1971. Used by permission of Tyndale House Publishers, Inc., Wheaton, Illinois 60189. All rights reserved.60189. All rights reserved.
Energy: Finding New Grace for the Pace

ISBN: 978-160683-975-1

Copyright © Beth Ann Jones

www.jeffandbethjones.org

Published by:
Harrison House Publishers
Tulsa, OK 74145

www.harrisonhouse.com

Printed in the United States of America. All rights reserved under International Copyright Law. Contents and/or cover may not be reproduced in whole or in part in any form without the express written consent of the Publisher.

CONTENTS

CHAPTER 1
FRIED OR ENERGIZED?

Overloaded, stressed and busy—I don't need to tell you—life is moving at a rapid pace these days! How are you handling it? Are you feeling fried or energized? With so many demands, choices and obligations, not to mention all the technology coming at us from every side, it can be overwhelming!

Before we know it, we are glazed over, operating on fumes and behaving like the hamster on the wheel.

Like you, I know that feeling. Back in the day, when we were pioneering a church and raising four preschoolers, I felt overloaded and stretched to my limit. The candle was burning at both ends and we were pedaling as fast as we could to keep pace with our season of life. I needed help! There were numerous mornings that I awoke and as soon as my feet hit the floor, all I could say and sing was an old hymn about grace, *"Thank you Lord for grace for the pace. 'Grace, grace, God's grace, grace that is greater than all our sin'. Lord, I thank You for grace."* I literally lived by those words. Through making that simple, heartfelt declaration of faith, I believe I tapped into something supernatural and accessed God's grace to help me in that season.

God understands the times we live in. Jesus experienced the busy, non-stop life of demands during His own life and ministry on earth. He knew that we would face pressures and stress. The question is: How does He want us to handle spinning all the plates or juggling every ball thrown at us?

Let's Visit Hamsterville

Mr. and Mrs. Hamster have been living this type of life for a long time. They are trying to please one another, their kids, their boss, and their employees—while also being Super Hamsters. As soon as dawn breaks, they find themselves up and on the spinning wheel of life—going round and round, faster and faster. Daddy Hamster's day begins before the crack of dawn. He showers, shaves, gulps down a skinny, dry *Hammuccinno,* and off to work he goes. He works hard all day, meeting with mice, guinea pigs and gerbils. He has to plan, make decisions, solve problems and make a profit. He pushes his body to the limit . . . spinning the wheel faster, faster and faster.

By five o'clock, he's beat. As he heads home to see the Mrs. and his little hammies, he dreams about resting on his Aspen shavings while the kids bring him his favorite plant roots. Unfortunately, when he arrives home he finds that Mrs. Hamster and the little hammies also had a busy day and they need his full, energetic attention. From dinnertime to bedtime, he's on full-time "daddy duty." Just before bed, he checks his email, sends a few texts, posts a pic to Hamigram and finally relaxes as he flips through the channels to catch up on Animal Planet. What a day! And just think— he gets to do it all over again tomorrow! Sound familiar?

Momma Ham has a busy life too. She wakes up early to the pitter-patter of little paws. She sets out the seeds, packs lunches and begins her chauffeuring duties as she hops into her gas-guzzling Hammer and drops off her little ones at school. She stops by the salon to get a *hamicure* and when she arrives back home at the cage, she spends the rest of the day cleaning up droppings, washing the wheel and using her mental, emotional and physical energy spinning around. By six o'clock, everyone is home and the night schedule kicks in. Momma Ham helps a few kids with their *hamwork,* while dad coaches the others in *wheel-spinning* practice. By midnight, Mr. and Mrs. Hamster are ready to collapse in a pile of shavings.

Can you relate to The Hamsters? Life is busy. Keeping up with the Hamsters can lead to physical, mental, emotional and spiritual burn out.

Help – I Need More Energy!

What does God have to say about all of this? How does He want us to manage our lives and energy? Is it possible to live life at a healthy pace and within a balanced margin? Is it possible to raise a family, maintain a home, work a successful job and serve the Lord without burning out? Unfortunately, many people are pressured to operate with zero margin— emotionally, physically, financially, and spiritually. And it's taking a toll!

The daily emotional quotient required for financial pressures, caring for aging parents, protecting our kids, watching out for terrorists and staying healthy is a major drain on our lives. Then add to this the need to keep up technologically! The Internet, as wonderful as it is, has opened up an entirely new set of pressures "to know." Information overload is taxing. Technology is changing at such a rapid rate that it takes three weeks just to research which television to buy. That's stress!

For Christians, there is an added degree of pressure. Believers are expected to be Christ-like at all times, to love their enemies and volunteer for charitable service, while at the same time being pressured into political-correctness. They are expected to rejoice when they are persecuted, mocked, laughed at or criticized for their faith in Jesus Christ. It can be overwhelming!

Grace for the Pace

You get the picture. Psychologists, physicians and researchers could tell you more from the secular angle and psychological angle, but what about the spiritual component? I've discovered that without knowing about, recognizing or tapping into the spiritual side of things, specifically God's "grace for the pace, it is impossible to keep up in this stressed and overloaded life. So, as we launch into this study, let's talk about and define grace for the pace.

> NUGGET: What is "grace for the pace?" What does it look like? There are many definitions for grace. Many times it's described as something spiritually ethereal. But grace is not a theory; it's tangible. Grace is a tangible spiritual commodity. God in His goodness gives us His grace to energize, empower and enable us in ways that we are unable to do through our own efforts, abilities or works.

Grace: Grace is from the Greek word, charis. There are many definitions for this rich word. Perhaps you've heard the grace acrostic: "God's Riches At Christ's Expense." According to Greek scholars, the word "grace" has meanings that include divine influence upon the heart, and its reflection in life; including gratitude. Grace is also translated as benefit, gift and favor.[1]

Grace is also seen as that kindness by which God bestows favors upon the ill-deserving, grants sinners pardon of their offences and bids them to accept eternal salvation through Christ. Grace is used of the merciful kindness by which God, exerting His holy influence upon souls, turns them to Christ, keeps, strengthens, increases them in Christian faith, knowledge, affection, and kindles them to the exercise of the Christian virtues.[2]

God's grace is manifold. The Bible describes at least three different categories of grace: *saving grace, standing grace and serving grace.*

Saving grace is the grace God gives to sinners to influence their hearts and turn them to Christ. We cannot be saved apart from God's grace. *"For it is by grace you have been saved, through faith - and this not from yourselves, it is the gift of God - not by works, so that no one can boast"* (Ephesians 2:8-9, NIV). Think about your own salvation. Do you remember how God graced you in such a way that you were able to have faith to believe? God's saving grace allows us to have faith to believe and be saved. It's truly a gift!

Standing grace is the grace God gives us to stand in faith and live the Christian life. We need God's grace to live. Romans 5:1-2 tells us, *"Therefore, since we have been justified through faith, we have peace with God through our Lord Jesus Christ, through whom we have gained access by faith into this grace in which we now stand" (NIV).* Through faith we stand in grace. God's standing grace gives us His ability to live in a place of rest and to have faith, to know, to grow, to think, to give, to be and to do all the things God wants for us. I would venture to say that most believers are unfamiliar with standing grace, but it is this very grace that we are talking about when we seek the Lord for "grace for the pace." When God gives us standing grace, He gives us His power, energy and ability for various areas of our lives.

Serving grace is the grace God gives us to serve Him. He gives us grace gifts, talents, passions and callings that are unique to each one of us. God has graced or gifted each of us in a special way so we can serve Him in a powerful and fruitful manner. Whether your serving grace is in the area of leadership, hospitality, teaching, mercy, giving or some other area, God enables and equips you for serving by His grace. The Apostle Paul understood serving grace when he said, *"We have different gifts, according to the grace given us" (Romans 12:6, NIV).* He also said, *"But by the grace of God I am what I am, and his grace to me was not without effect. No, I worked harder than all of them-yet not I, but the grace of God that was with me" (1 Corinthians 15:10, NIV).* Notice that Paul said that it was the grace of God within him that allowed him to work and serve God. Each one of us has been endowed with serving grace that also helps us function in the "grace for the pace."

I believe that one of the most powerful promises in the Bible is Romans 5:17: *"For if, by the trespass of the one man, death reigned through that one man, how much more will those who receive God's abundant provision of grace and of the gift of righteousness reign in life through the one man, Jesus Christ" (NIV).*

When we truly receive God's abundant provision of grace—saving grace, standing grace and serving grace—along with His gift of righteousness, we can reign in life. What does it mean to reign in life? It means that we are empowered to overcome every bit of stress and overload that is thrown our way. I encourage you to open your heart as we study the power of God's grace for the pace.

> NUGGET: Simply put: Grace for the pace is when God Almighty gives us a supernatural deposit or endowment of inner strength, energy, gifting, ability, know-how, understanding, knowledge and favor which first leads us to salvation and then helps us stand in victory and serve God. God's grace helps us with the pace—the stressed and overloaded lives we often face. We need God's grace for the pace. Grace is His free gift to man. What a gift—that God Almighty would impart His grace to us and that grace would supernaturally help us succeed in whatever we face! When we truly receive God's grace for the pace, we receive the ability to function at the pace required of us.

Living in the grace of God is to receive, recognize and identify our God-given gifts and bents, and connect them with the God-given season and callings in our lives. Like a glove and hand, God's grace and our life work together in a supernatural rhythm. In practical terms, grace for the pace is when God graces us with *His ability, His power and His energy* to be the Christian wife, husband, mom, dad, friend, businessperson, entrepreneur, athlete, builder, engineer, doctor, lawyer, homemaker, manager, chef, clerk, pastor, evangelist, coach, volunteer, banker, baker, candlestick maker or whatever He's called us to be!

If you have grace . . . life is like a well-greased machine. There's a flow. There's supernatural ease. You know when to say *yes,* and when to say *no.* Whatever you need to know, be, or do—God wants to grace you in such a way that you have His supernatural ability in that area. Grace is huge! Can you see how wonderful God's grace is?

> **NUGGET:** On the other side of the coin, without grace you will eventually burn out and resent the very things you once loved. Without grace you'll do what you have to do, but eventually you'll start to feel like a "flat-liner" in life and experience a sense of detachment. *Without grace, you function but there's no unction. You survive, but you do not thrive. You may be skilled, but you are not fulfilled. You live and die, but never know why.* Get the picture? Without God's grace for the pace, there will be sorrow and regret in the end.

Now, let's dive into God's Word to see what He has to say about stress and overloaded lives.

The Need for Speed

1. John 16:33

    Underline the phrase "in Me you may have peace."

    > *These things I have spoken to you, that in Me you may have peace. In the world you will have tribulation; but be of good cheer, I have overcome the world. (NKJV).*

    What did Jesus promise we would have in this world?

    Jesus said we would face stress and overload in this life. The word "tribulation" comes from the Greek word *thlipsis*, which literally and figuratively means "pressure." It's also translated as anguish, burden, trouble, persecution.[3] In other words, stress and overload!

Describe a time you felt anguished, burdened, troubled, persecuted or pressured.

What did Jesus tell us to do in response to pressure?

What does Jesus promise us in Him?

2.   Proverbs 24:10

Underline the word that describes stress.

> *If you fail under pressure, your strength is not very great. (NLT).*

What is the purpose of pressure, busyness and stress? → *guilt*
get things done

If we cave in to pressure, what does this tell us about ourselves?

NUGGET: This is a wake-up call. The enemy's goal is for us to get so busy, pressured, stressed and overwhelmed that we lose touch with God and our vital personal relationship with Him, and fail in life's endeavors. It's important for us to be strong in the Lord and continually strengthen our inner man so our emotional, mental and physical life will be energized, enabling us to overcome in life.

3.   Luke 10:38-42

Underline the phrases "Martha [overly occupied and too busy] was distracted" and "Martha, Martha, you are anxious and troubled about many things."

> *Now while they were on their way, it occurred that Jesus entered a certain village, and a woman named Martha received and welcomed Him into her house. And she had a sister named Mary, who seated herself at the Lord's feet and was listening to His teaching. But Martha [overly occupied and too busy] was distracted with much serving; and she came up to Him and said, Lord, is it nothing to You that my sister has left me to serve alone? Tell her then to help me [to lend a hand and do her part along with me]! But the Lord replied to her by saying, Martha, Martha, you are anxious and troubled about many things; There is need of only one or but a few things. Mary has chosen the good portion [that which is to her advantage], which shall not be taken away from her (AMP).*

This is such a great story because we can all relate to it. Most of us want to be Mary, but many of us are like Martha.

What type of person was Martha?

What type of person was Mary?

Which one are you?

13

What was Martha's priority?

What was Mary's priority?

Who had more stress?

Why was Martha so stressed out?

We often live like Martha at work, at home and in ministry. Jesus loved Martha, but He had to set her straight. Jesus clarified the difference between "many things" and "one thing."

What are the "many things" that distract and pressure you?

What is the "one thing" Jesus said was needed?

What do you think the phrase "one thing is needed" means?

The biggest secret of this story is found in the last verse. What did Mary do?

Describe the challenge of "choosing" in your own life.

Type A Marthas:

Do you think Martha may have been a Type A personality?

According to psychologist Shelly Wu, Ph.D, these traits fit the Type A personality:[4]

Type A people are always on the move.

Type A people have a strong sense of urgency.

Type A people often sit at the edge of their seats, literally.

Type A people check their watches more frequently.

Type A people are often obsessed with their work.

Type A people are extremely competitive.

Type A people want to get things done and they will do almost anything to accomplish their goals.

Type A people tend to become aggressive, impatient, and irritable at anyone or anything that interferes with their work.

Type A people are more likely to get heart disease. Once they have the disease, they are more likely to diligently follow their doctors' orders. Therefore, they are also more likely to recover from the disease.

Does this describe you? In what ways?

 4. James 1:10

Underline the last sentence.

> *But a rich man should be glad that his riches mean nothing to the Lord, for he will soon be gone, like a flower that has lost its beauty and fades away, withered-killed by the scorching summer sun. So it is with rich men. They will soon die and leave behind all their busy activities (TLB).*

Putting things in perspective is always a good idea. What does this verse tell us about the end result of all our busy pursuits?

Jesus said, *"For what will it profit a man if he gains the whole world, and loses his own soul?" (Mark 8:36, NKJV).* If busyness, pressures, stress and overload cause us to lose perspective and misplace our priorities, we are missing it.

NUGGET: Be aware of the temptation to become so busy in your own pursuits that seeking God and His Church gets squeezed right out of your life. It's a formula for disaster. When people put their job, kids' sports, travel, hobbies, education, sleep and personal projects in the slot reserved for God alone, they run the risk of facing personal, marital, business and health problems. We all face this temptation. Sadly, we've watched many families over the years get busy with successful careers, educational pursuits, fitness goals and children's sporting or extracurricular activities, and put Jesus on the back burner as their church attendance became less and less

frequent. The most heartbreaking result is seeing people go through difficulties that have taken a huge toll on their lives. God wants to protect you from going down that road.

Jesus told us, *"But seek first the kingdom of God and His righteousness, and all these things shall be added to you" (Matthew 6:33, NKJV).* When we seek God first, He gives us the grace and blessings that go along with His kingdom.

5.   Second Corinthians 4:8-9

Underline the words "hard pressed," "perplexed," "persecuted" and "struck down."

> *We are hard-pressed on every side, yet not crushed; we are perplexed, but not in despair; persecuted, but not forsaken; struck down, but not destroyed (NKJV).*

This passage describes the "almost breaking" point of stress and pressure. What four words describe stress and pressure?

In what areas of your life do you feel these pressures?

What four words describe our ability to stand strong?

6.   Psalm 61:2

Underline the phrase "when my heart is overwhelmed."

From the end of the earth I will cry to You, when my heart is overwhelmed; lead me to the rock that is higher than I (NKJV).

What do we do when we feel overwhelmed?

Who is the Rock?

If you are overwhelmed, run to the Rock! Jesus is the Rock, and we can always run to Him. Perhaps you need to spend some time just getting quiet, praying, listening to worship music and reading your Bible. Let your heart settle in with Him.

Slow Down

We live in the hurry-up world. Doctors have even identified "hurry-up syndrome!" The term *hurry sickness* was coined back in the 1950s when cardiologists Meyer Friedman and Ray Rosenman were researching personality types. By 1959, they had refined this to the now classic Type A personality, a key element of which was a "harrying sense of time urgency."[5]

> NUGGET: In his book, *Faster: The Acceleration of Just About Everything*, James Gleick describes the fact that never in the history of the human race have so many had so much to do in so little time.[6] He says, *"Most of us suffer some degree of 'hurry sickness,' a malady that has launched us into the 'epoch of the nanosecond,' a need-everything-yesterday sphere dominated by cell phones, computers, faxes, and remote controls. Yet for all the hours, minutes, and even seconds being saved, we're still filling our days to the point that we have no time for such basic human activities as eating, sex, and relating to our families."*

The Hurried Woman Syndrome is affecting as many as 30 million women each year, according to Dr. Brent W. Bost's book by the same title.7 The Hurried Woman Syndrome can drain your energy, cause you to gain weight (or have trouble keeping your weight stable), increase your moodiness and frustration, and lower your sexual energy as well.

According to Dr. Bost, the three major symptoms of the Hurried Woman Syndrome are:

Fatigue or a low mood

Weight gain

Low sex drive (libido)

He goes on to say that, " ... *women, usually between the ages of 25 and 55 and often with children between the ages of 4 and 16, are most often affected by the Hurried Woman Syndrome. Many Hurried Women work outside the home, but a large number of women who suffer with the syndrome stay at home. Even women who don't have children can come down with it—a stressful career, sick relative, or burdensome responsibilities can all contribute to making the symptoms worse. Stress is probably the single most important factor that causes women to complain about the Hurried Woman Syndrome. There are many types of stress and they vary from patient to patient. Sometimes the stress can't be avoided, such as a sick child or a high-powered career. However, for the majority of women, much of the stress is avoidable or at least could be managed better. These avoidable stresses are those that often come from a busy, hectic schedule and lifestyle choices that many of us have embraced as completely normal. Yet, the effects of this kind of stress— what I call hurry— can have very significant long-term and wide-reaching consequences for the woman who labors under it and those around her who suffer along with her.*"

Does God have answers to the hurry-up world we live in? Of course! We see in the Word that there are legitimate times to hurry—when God tells you to run, to escape danger, to tell the good news, or things of this nature. We also see that those who live by faith don't make haste; there is a degree of patience and the ability to wait on the Lord that is healthy and godly.

1.   Jeremiah 2:25

Underline the reason people were in a hurry.

Slow down. Take a deep breath. What's the hurry? Why wear yourself out? Just what are you after anyway? But you say, 'I can't help it. I'm addicted to alien gods. I can't quit' (The Message).

There are many "gods" pulling for our affection, time and attention.

What are the alien gods in your life?

NUGGET: Let's talk about alien gods in today's culture. Unfortunately, one of the biggest alien gods that families worship is sports. Basketball practice, hockey ice time, soccer tournaments and the like have invaded every day of the week, including Sunday mornings.

As a result, many parents are teaching their children how to worship athletics instead of Jesus Christ. Parents wear themselves out trying to get their children to practice and travel team games, secretly hoping that it produces a full-ride college scholarship for their child at the expense of their spiritual life. Of course, the occasional game or tournament arises and sometimes cannot be helped, but for many families, it's not "occasional," it's "regular."

Then when their kids hit the teen years, parents say things like: *"I don't know why my son or daughter just doesn't like church or youth group.*

They said it's not fun. I'm not going to make them go, it's their choice." The reason teens don't like church or youth group is because parents have inadvertently taught their kids not to value those things. When parents train their kids to worship alien gods (sports, popularity, etc.), they won't have the desire to worship the Living God unless it's "fun" or "cool." Isn't that sad? (Not that church and youth group isn't or can't be fun and cool.) Why do parents give their kids a choice when it comes to attending church and youth group when they would never dream of giving that same child the choice of attending a sports practice or game? Alien gods.

Alien gods include anything we put in front of the living God. They can be anything we worship. If we're not careful, golfing, gardening, sleeping, boating, skiing, the cottage or "my time" can become an alien god. God does want us to enjoy life, recreation and His Creation, but not at the expense of our spiritual condition. If any alien god is taking His place, eating up His time and spending His money, then it's time to slow down and return to the King of kings and the Lord of lords.

2.   Isaiah 28:16

Underline the phrase "whoever believes will not act hastily."

> *Therefore thus says the Lord God: "Behold, I lay in Zion a stone for a foundation, a tried stone, a precious cornerstone, a sure foundation; whoever believes will not act hastily (NKJV).*

Jesus is the precious Cornerstone and our sure Foundation. This verse tells us that he who believes in Him as their sure foundation will not be given to do what?

The idea is that there is a rest for the believer. They do not need to panic, hurry or be dismayed in any way. Their faith in Jesus Christ provides stability.

3.　　　　Proverbs 28:20

Underline the results of being too hasty.

> *A faithful man will abound with blessings, but he who hastens*
> *to be rich will not go unpunished (NKJV).*

What is this person hurrying to do?

What's the difference between a "faithful man" and one who "hastens
to be rich"?

What is the result of the person who hurries to be rich?

There are some things we do need to be in a "hurry" to do. What are
those things, according to the following verses?

-Psalm 119:60, *"I made haste, and did not delay to keep Your*
commandments" (NKJV)

-Luke 19:5, *When Jesus got to the tree, he looked up and said,*
"Zacchaeus, hurry down. Today is my day to be a guest in your home
(The Message).

-Isaiah 26:7-8, *The path of right-living people is level. The Leveler evens*
the road for the right-living. We're in no hurry, GOD. We're content to
linger in the path sign-posted with your decisions. Who you are and
what you've done are all we'll ever want (The Message).

-Isaiah 40:28-31, *Have you never heard or understood? Don't you know that the LORD is the everlasting God, the Creator of all the earth? He never grows faint or weary. No one can measure the depths of his understanding. He gives power to those who are tired and worn out; he offers strength to the weak. Even youths will become exhausted, and young men will give up. But those who wait on the LORD will find new strength. They will fly high on wings like eagles. They will run and not grow weary. They will walk and not faint" (NLT).*

Satan's Meeting

This e-mail about busyness, written by Charles A. Beard was passed around the Internet many years ago and it's still worth a read:

Satan called a worldwide convention of demons. In his opening address, he said "We can't keep Christians from going to church. We can't keep them from reading their bibles and knowing the truth. We can't even keep them from forming an intimate relationship with their Savior. Once they gain that connection with Jesus, our power over them is broken. So let them go to their churches. Let them have their covered dish dinners, but steal their time so they don't have time to develop a relationship with Jesus Christ. This is what I want you to do," said the devil. "Distract them from gaining hold of their Savior and maintaining that vital connection throughout their day!"

"How shall we do this?" his demons shouted.

"Keep them busy in the nonessentials of life and invent innumerable schemes to occupy their minds," he answered. "Tempt them to spend, spend, spend and borrow, borrow, borrow. Persuade the wives to go to work for long hours and the husbands to work 6-7 days each week, 10-12 hrs a day, so they can afford their empty lifestyles. Keep them from spending time with their children. As their families begin to fragment, soon their homes will offer no escape from

the pressures of work! Over stimulate their minds so they cannot hear that still small voice. Entice them to play the radio whenever they drive, and to keep the TV, VCR, CD's, and their PC's going constantly in their home. See to it that every store and restaurant in the world plays non-biblical music constantly. This will jam their minds and break that union with Christ. Fill the coffee tables with magazines and newspapers. Pound their minds with the news 24 hours a day. Invade their driving moments with billboards, flood their mailboxes with junk mail and mail order catalogs, sweepstakes, and every kind of newsletter and promotional offering free products, services and false hopes. Keep skinny beautiful models on the magazines and TV so their husbands will believe that outward beauty is what's important, and they'll become dissatisfied with their wives.

Keep the wives too tired to love their husbands at night. Give them headaches, too! If they don't give their husbands the love they need, they will begin to look elsewhere. That will fragment their families quickly! Give them Santa Claus to distract them from teaching their children the real meaning of Christmas. Give them an Easter Bunny so they won't talk about His resurrection and power over sin and death. Even in their recreation, let them be excessive. Have them return from their recreation exhausted. Keep them too busy to go out in nature and reflect on God's creation.

Send them to amusement parks, sporting events, plays, concerts, and movies instead. Keep them busy, busy, busy! And when they meet for spiritual fellowship, involve them in gossip and small talk so that they leave with troubled consciences. Crowd their lives with so many good causes, so they will have no time to seek power from Jesus. Soon they will be working on their own strength, sacrificing their health and family for the good of the cause. It will work! It will work!"

It was quite a plan! The demons went eagerly to their assignments causing Christians everywhere to get more busy and more rushed, going here and there, having little time for God and their families, having no time to tell others about the power of Jesus to change lives. I guess the question is, "Has the devil been successful at his scheme?" You be the judge!

God has a better plan! If you've felt like a busy, stressed-out and overloaded hamster on the wheel, it's time to enter into God's rest and tap into His grace for the pace. Hebrew 4:3 says, *"For we which have believed do enter into rest (KJV).*

Scriptures to Meditate On

"Be still, and know that I am God:

I will be exalted among the heathen,

I will be exalted in the earth."

Psalm 46:10, KJV

"For we which have believed do enter into rest"

Hebrews 4:3, KJV

Group Discussion

Describe the pace of your own life. What plates are you required to spin and how many balls do you have to juggle?

Describe your experience with God's saving, standing or serving grace.

Describe the things that tempt and distract you, causing you to lose the focus of your priorities. In your experience, what "alien gods" do you and those in our society struggle with?

----

[1] Biblesoft, Inc. and International Bible Translators, Inc. *New Exhaustive Strong's Numbers and Concordance with ExpandedGreek-Hebrew Dictionary.* Copyright © 1994, 2003

[2] Biblesoft, Inc., *Thayer's Greek Lexicon, Electronic Database.* Copyright (c) 2002, 2003, 2006, 2011

[3] Biblesoft, Inc. and International Bible Translators, Inc. *New Exhaustive Strong's Numbers and Concordance with Expanded Greek-Hebrew Dictionary.* Copyright © 1994, 2003.

[4] http://psychology.about.com/library/howto/httypea.htm

[5] http://www.wordspy.com/words/hurrysickness.asp

[6] Gleik, James, *Faster: The Acceleration of Just About Everything.* (New York: Pantheon Books, 1999).

[7] Bost, Brent W., *The Hurried Woman Syndrome.* (New York: McGraw-Hill, 2005).

CHAPTER 2
THE ENERGIZER BUNNY'S GOT NOTHING ON YOU

You've watched the Energizer Bunny, right? That little guy never runs out of energy. He just keeps on going and going and going. If a set of batteries can do that for a bunny, what can God's power and grace do for you?

God never intended for us to live life without help. We all face demands, and we need help! We need supernatural energy. Our good friend and minister, Tony Cooke, tells the often-repeated story of the bricklayer who could have used some extra help!

Trying to Do the Job Alone

Dear Sir:

I am writing in response to your request for additional information for my "trying to do the job alone" as the cause of my accident. You said in your letter that I should explain that statement more fully. I trust the following details will be sufficient.

I am a bricklayer by trade. On the date of the accident, I was working alone on the roof of a new six-story building. When I completed my work, I discovered that I had about 500 pounds of brick left over. Rather than carrying the bricks down by hand, I decided to lower them in a barrel by using a pulley which was attached to the side of the building at the sixth-floor level.

Securing the rope at ground level, I went up to the roof, swung the barrel out, and loaded the bricks into it. Then I went back to the ground and untied the rope, holding it tightly to insure a slow descent of the 500 pounds of bricks. You will note in block number 22 of the claim form that my weight is 150 pounds.

Due to my surprise at being jerked off the ground so suddenly, I lost my presence of mind and forgot to let go of the rope. Needless to say, I proceeded up the side of the building at a very rapid rate of speed. In the vicinity of the third floor, I met the barrel coming down. This explains my fractured skull and collarbone.

Slowed only slightly, I continued my rapid ascent, not stopping until the fingers of my right hand were two knuckles deep into the pulley. By this time, I had regained my presence of mind and was able to hold tightly to the rope in spite of my pain. At approximately the same time however, the barrel of bricks hit the ground and the bottom fell out of the barrel. Devoid of the weight of the bricks, the barrel then weighed approximately 50 pounds. I refer you again to the information in block number 22 regarding my weight. As you might imagine, I began a rapid descent down the side of the building. In the vicinity of the third floor, I met the barrel coming up. This accounts for the two fractured ankles and the lacerations of my legs and lower body. This second encounter with the barrel slowed me enough to lessen my injuries when I fell onto the pile of bricks, and fortunately, only three vertebrae were cracked.

I am sorry to report, however, that as I lay there on the bricks in pain, unable to stand, and watching the empty barrel six stories above me, I again lost my presence of mind and let go of the rope. The empty barrel weighed more than the rope, so it came down upon me and broke both of my legs.

I hope I have furnished information sufficient to explain why "trying to do the job alone" was the stated cause of the accident.

Sincerely,

A Bricklayer

NUGGET: Trying to do the job alone is not God's plan for us! Together, we are all more effective than any of us would be alone. When we realize that God has graced us to function as a team with those around us, life gets easier! In addition to the people God places in our lives to help us, He gives us grace to help us. Let's take some time to welcome Grace to our team!

God Gives You Grace to Help

1.   Hebrews 4:16

Underline the words "throne of grace" and "find grace to help."

> Let us therefore come boldly to the throne of grace, that we may obtain mercy and find grace to help in time of need (NKJV).

What does God call His very throne?

What can we obtain at God's throne?

mercy + find. grace to help

The Amplified Bible details this: *Let us then fearlessly and confidently and boldly draw near to the throne of grace (the throne of God's unmerited favor to us sinners), that we may receive mercy [for our failures] and find grace to help in good time for every need [appropriate help and well-timed help, coming just when we need it]. Hebrews 4:16, AMP*

According to this verse, what will grace do for you?

help in good time for every need

Notice this "grace to help" is there for our time of need.

How should you approach God's throne in order to receive "grace to help"?

fearlessly, confidently, boldly

Don't hesitate. Because of your relationship with Jesus Christ, you can approach God's throne of grace with boldness to receive His mercy and find grace to help you in every time of need, including times of stress, pressure and busyness.

Let's take a moment right now to receive more grace. *"Father, I am so thankful that because of the blood of Jesus Christ, the saving grace You've given to me, and my union with Him, I can come into Your Presence with boldness. You said I could obtain mercy and find grace to help at Your throne of grace and Father, I thank You for that. Right now, I appropriate Your mercy and grace and I ask You to impart a fresh dose of Your standing and serving grace into my life to help me in every arena. I thank You, Lord, that right now I believe I receive a deposit of grace from Your very throne. Thank You. In Jesus' Name. Amen."*

2.   Acts 27:1-44

Underline the word "helps." This is a long passage, but one that describes the reality of pressure and stress in living color. The Apostle Paul was in the storm of his life. If you've ever felt your boat rocking in the storms created by an overwhelmed life, you'll appreciate this story and see a simple principle that helped Paul during this storm.

And when it was determined that we should sail into Italy, they delivered Paul and certain other prisoners unto one named Julius, a centurion of Augustus' band. And entering into a ship of Adramyttium, we launched, meaning to sail by the coasts of Asia; one Aristarchus, a Macedonian of Thessalonica, being with us. And the next day we touched at Sidon. And Julius courteously entreated Paul, and gave him liberty to go unto his friends to refresh himself. And when we had launched from thence, we sailed under Cyprus, because the winds were contrary. And when we had sailed over the sea of Cilicia and Pamphylia, we came to Myra, a city of Lycia. And there the centurion found a ship of Alexandria sailing into Italy; and he put us therein. And when we had sailed slowly many days, and scarce were come over against Cnidus, the wind not suffering us, we sailed under Crete, over against Salmone; And, hardly passing it, came unto a place which is called The fair havens; nigh whereunto was the city of Lasea. Now when much time was spent, and when sailing was now dangerous, because the fast was now already past, Paul admonished them, And said unto them, Sirs, I perceive that this voyage will be with hurt and much damage, not only of the lading and ship, but also of our lives. Nevertheless the centurion believed the master and the owner of the ship, more than those things which were spoken by Paul. And because the haven was not commodious to winter in, the more part advised to depart thence also, if by any means they might attain to Phenice, and there to winter; which is an haven of Crete, and lieth toward the south west and north west. And when the south wind blew softly, supposing that they had obtained their purpose, loosing thence, they sailed close by Crete. But not long after there arose against it a tempestuous wind, called Euroclydon. And when the ship was caught, and could not bear up into the wind, we let her drive. And running under a certain island which is called Clauda, we had much work to come by the boat: Which when they had taken up, they used helps, undergirding the ship; and, fearing lest they should fall into the quicksands, strake sail, and so were driven. And we being exceedingly tossed with a tempest, the next day they lightened the ship; And the third day we cast out with our own hands the tackling of the ship. And when neither sun nor stars in many days appeared, and no small tempest lay on us, all hope that we should be saved was then taken away. But after long abstinence Paul stood forth in the midst of them, and said, Sirs, ye should have hearkened unto me, and not have loosed from Crete, and to have gained this harm and loss. And now I exhort you to be of good cheer: for there shall be no loss of any man's life among you, but of the ship. For there stood by me this night the angel of God, whose I am, and whom I serve, Saying, Fear not, Paul; thou must be brought before Caesar: and, lo, God hath given thee all them that sail with thee. Wherefore, sirs, be of good cheer: for I believe God, that it shall be even as it was told me. Howbeit we must be cast upon a certain island. But when the fourteenth night was come, as we were driven up and down in Adria, about midnight the shipmen deemed that they drew near to some country; And sounded, and found it twenty fathoms: and when they had gone a little further, they sounded again, and found it fifteen fathoms. Then fearing lest we should have fallen upon rocks, they cast four anchors out of the stern, and wished for the day. And as the shipmen were about to flee out of the ship, when they had let down the boat into the sea, under colour as though they would have cast anchors out of the foreship, Paul said to the centurion and to the soldiers, Except these abide in the ship, ye cannot be saved. Then the soldiers cut off the ropes of the boat, and let her fall off. And while the day was coming on, Paul besought them all to take meat, saying, This day is the fourteenth day that ye have tarried and continued fasting, having taken nothing. Wherefore I pray you to take some meat: for this is for your health: for there shall not an hair fall from the head of any of you. And when he had thus spoken, he took bread, and gave thanks to God in presence of them all: and when he had broken it, he began to eat. Then were they all of good cheer, and they also took some meat. And we were in all in work to come by the boat: Which when they had taken up, they used helps, undergirding the ship; and, fearing lest they should fall into the quicksands, strake sail, and so were driven. And we being exceedingly tossed with a tempest, the next day they lightened the ship; And the third day we cast out with our own hands the tackling of the ship. And when neither sun nor stars in many days appeared, and no small tempest lay on us, all hope that we should be saved was then taken away. But after long abstinence Paul stood forth in the midst of them, and said, Sirs, ye should have hearkened unto me, and not have loosed from Crete, and to have gained this harm and loss. And now I exhort you to be of good cheer: for there shall be no loss of any man's life among you, but of the ship. For there stood by me this night the angel of God, whose I am, and whom I serve, Saying, Fear not, Paul; thou must be brought before Caesar: and, lo, God hath given thee all them that sail with thee. Wherefore, sirs, be of good cheer: for I believe God, that it shall be even as it was told me. Howbeit we must be cast upon a certain island. But when the fourteenth night was come, as we were driven up and down in Adria, about midnight the shipmen deemed that they drew near to some country; And sounded, *and found it twenty fathoms: and when they had gone a little further, they sounded again, and found it fifteen fathoms. Then fearing lest we should have fallen upon rocks, they cast four anchors out of the stern, and wished for the day. And as the shipmen were about to flee out of the ship, when they had let down the boat into the sea, under colour as though they would have cast anchors out of the foreship, Paul said to the centurion and to the soldiers, Except these abide in the ship, ye cannot be saved. Then the soldiers cut off the ropes of the boat, and let her fall off. And while the day was coming on, Paul besought them all to take meat, saying, This day is the fourteenth day that ye have tarried and continued fasting, having taken nothing. Wherefore I pray you to take some meat: for this is for your health: for there shall not an hair fall from the head of any of you. And when he had thus spoken, he took bread, and gave thanks to God in presence of them all: and when he had broken it, he began to eat. 36 Then were they all of good cheer, and they also took some meat. And we were in all in the ship two hundred threescore and sixteen souls. And when they had eaten enough, they lightened the ship, and cast out the wheat into the sea. And when it was day, they knew not the land: but they discovered a certain creek with a shore, into the which they were minded, if it were possible, to thrust in the ship. And when they had taken up the anchors, they committed themselves unto the sea, and loosed the rudder bands, and hoised up the mainsail to the wind, and made toward shore. And falling into a place where two seas met, they ran the ship aground; and the forepart stuck fast, and remained unmoveable, but the hinder part was broken with the violence of the waves. And the soldiers' counsel was to kill the prisoners, lest any of them should swim out, and escape. But the centurion, willing to save Paul, kept them from their purpose; and commanded that they which could swim should cast themselves first into the sea, and get to land: And the rest, some on boards, and some on broken pieces of the ship. And so it came to pass, that they escaped all safe to land. KJV*

What did Paul perceive about his journey?

What type of storm did Paul face?

When the boat was reeling in the waves and about to be broken up by the fierce storm, what did they do to reinforce and strengthen the ship?

used helps

NUGGET: The King James Bible tells us they used "helps" to undergird the ship. These helps were giant ropes onboard the ship. The sailors wrapped and undergirded the ship with these giant ropes to help strengthen the boat and to keep it from falling apart in the storm. These ropes helped keep the ship together in a time of stress. That's what grace does! When we face life's storms, choppy waters, never-ending pressure and we feel like we are about to fall apart, God's grace undergirds us. In the very same way, God's grace helps us in the midst of storms, stress and pressure. He wraps us up in His grace ropes and strengthens us.

3.　　Zechariah 4:7

Underline the words we are to shout.

Who are you, O great mountain? Before Zerubbabel you shall become a plain! And he shall bring forth the capstone with shouts of "Grace, grace to it! (NKJV).

What did they cry out against the obstacles and mountains that stood in their way? Have you shouted grace to the mountains of stress and obstacles of overload in your life by faith?

God offers you real, tangible grace to help you in your time of need. When you're feeling overwhelmed, overloaded and overstressed, there is grace to help. Start shouting!

God Gives You People to Help

1. Exodus 18:13-26

In this lengthy passage, underline verses 14, 18, 21 and 23.

13 The next day Moses took his seat to serve as judge for the people, and they stood around him from morning till evening. 14 When his father-in-law saw all that Moses was doing for the people, he said, "What is this you are doing for the people? Why do you alone sit as judge, while all these people stand around you from morning till evening?" 15 Moses answered him, "Because the people come to me to seek God's will. 16 Whenever they have a dispute, it is brought to me, and I decide between the parties and inform them of God's decrees and laws." 17 Moses' father-in-law replied, "What you are doing is not good. 18 You and these people who come to you will only wear yourselves out. The work is too heavy for you; you cannot handle it alone. 19 Listen now to me and I will give you some advice, and may God be with you. You must be the people's representative before God and bring their disputes to him. 20 Teach them the decrees and laws, and show them the way to live and the duties they are to perform. 21 But select capable men from all the people — men who fear God, trustworthy men who hate dishonest gain — and appoint them as officials over thousands, hundreds, fifties and tens. 22 Have them serve as judges for the people at all times, but have them bring every difficult case to you; the simple cases they can decide themselves. That will make your load lighter, because they will share it with you. 23 If you do this and God so commands, you will be able to stand the strain, and all these people will go home satisfied." 24 Moses listened to his father-in-law and did everything he said. 25 He chose capable men from all Israel and made them leaders of the people, officials over thousands, hundreds, fifties and tens. 26 They served as judges for the people at all times. The difficult cases they brought to Moses, but the simple ones they decided themselves (NIV).

It's a reality that you and I cannot do it all alone. We need help! Moses faced this overload challenge and was finally given godly counsel from his father-in-law.

What was Moses trying to do by himself?

serve as judge

What did Moses' father-in-law tell him about this unhealthy practice?

It is not good

What does verse 17 tell us about doing this alone?

Trying to do it all by yourself is too heavy a load to carry. It's not God's plan. We need help. Do you believe that God will connect you with people who will be a help to you and those whom you can help?

What did God's counsel look like?

a group of capable men who fear God + are trustworthy)

In the end, what kind of people did God use to help Moses?

L

What does verse 23 promise us if we get help?

will be able to stand the strain

2.   Numbers 11:11-17

Underline verses 14 and 17.

> 11 And Moses said to the LORD, "Why are you treating me, your servant, so miserably? What did I do to deserve the burden of a people like this? 12 Are they my children? Am I their father? Is that why you have told me to carry them in my arms — like a nurse carries a baby — to the land you swore to give their ancestors? 13 Where am I supposed to get meat for all these people? They keep complaining and saying, 'Give us meat!' 14 I can't carry all these people by myself! The load is far too heavy! 15 I'd rather you killed me than treat me like this. Please spare me this misery!" 16 Then the LORD said to Moses, "Summon before me seventy of the leaders of Israel. Bring them to the Tabernacle to stand there with you. 17 I will come down and talk to you there. I will take some of the Spirit that is upon you, and I will put the Spirit upon them also. They will

bear the burden of the people along with you, so you will not have to carry it alone (NLT).

Moses was feeling the heavy load of leading the people of Israel and realized that he could not do it alone.

What did Moses tell the Lord in verse 14?

What did Moses ask the Lord for?

What was the Lord's response?

We need godly relief to overcome overloaded lives. If you sometimes feel that the load you carry is too much for you, begin to believe God for divine connections and the right people to come into your life to help you in whatever area you require help.

God Gives You Wisdom and Peace to Help

1.   Psalm 29:11

Underline the phrases "God makes" and "God gives."

GOD makes his people strong. GOD gives his people peace. The Message

What does God make? *people strong*

What does God give? *peace*

2.   Proverbs 3:13-18

Underline the words "wisdom" and "understanding."

> *Happy is the man who finds <u>wisdom</u>, and the man who gains <u>understanding</u>; For her proceeds are better than the profits of silver, and her gain than fine gold. She is more precious than rubies, and all the things you may desire cannot compare with her. Length of days is in her right hand, in her left hand riches and honor. Her ways are ways of pleasantness, and all her paths are peace. She is a tree of life to those who take hold of her, and happy are all who retain her (NKJV).*

List all the things God promises to us when we walk in wisdom and understanding:

3.   John 14:27, 16:33

Underline the word "peace."

> *Peace I leave with you, My <u>peace</u> I give to you; not as the world gives do I give to you. Let not your heart be troubled, neither let it be afraid (John 14:27, NKJV)*

> *These things I have spoken to you, that in Me you may have <u>peace</u>. In the world you will have tribulation; but be of good cheer, I have overcome the world (John 16:33, NKJV)*

What did Jesus promise us?

Scriptures to Meditate On

"So do not fear, for I am with you;

do not be dismayed, for I am your God.

I will strengthen you and help you;

I will uphold you and with my righteous right hand."

Isaiah 41:10, NIV

"God is our refuge and strength,

A very present help in trouble."

Psalm 46:1, NKJV

Group Discussion

1. Describe a time you tried to do a job alone. How was it? Have you looked at the team of people God has placed around you? Have you considered seeking or hiring help? Have you welcomed grace to your team? Describe this.

2. Describe the way you have experienced God's grace helping, energizing or strengthening you—like the ropes that undergirded and strengthened the Apostle Paul's ship.

3. Describe an area in your life where you need more grace to help.

CHAPTER 3
RECHARGING

I don't know about you, but marathoners impress me. A few years ago my husband Jeff, along with 35,000 others, ran the Chicago Marathon. I was so proud of him! As I watched the runners, I noticed that they all paced themselves. As soon as the starting gun goes off, everyone starts with a rush of adrenaline and energy, yet they realize they cannot keep this starting pace if they want to finish the race. As my husband expended more and more energy during the race, he needed to be recharged and replenished. He needed glucose and water to continually energize and hydrate his body so he wouldn't wear out before he reached the finish line. It would have been crazy for him to presume to run the race at his own pace without some type of relief along the way.

As we stood in the grandstands that day watching everyone cross the finish line of the Chicago Marathon, I had a God moment. I thought, *Lord, this is what You see every day. People finish their race on earth and they cross that heavenly finish line.* Some of those in the Chicago Marathon finished the race strong, energized and full of joy. Many finished with a limp or a stagger, while others crawled across the finish line. No matter how they came in, that finish line was a place of joy and celebration!

In the same way, we are all running our God-given race. We need God's grace to help us keep the pace and finish our race! We need His grace for the pace to keep us strengthened and replenished for our entire lifetime. His grace brings us the relief we need in our race. God wants all of us to finish our race of faith with joy.

We Need to Be Recharged

Bill Hybels, senior pastor of Willowcreek Church, shares a great illustration about three gauges we need to pay attention to: our physical gauge, emotional gauge and spiritual gauge. Throughout our lives, these gauges are in constant use and we need to be intentional about replenishing them. We cannot run on empty. It's important to be recharged and to refuel.

How are your gauges? Is your spiritual gauge on full? Where is the needle on your emotional gauge? Is your physical gauge showing a full charge?

Psalm 23:3

Underline the part of you God promises to restore.

> *... he restores my soul. He guides me in paths of righteousness for his name's sake. NIV*

What does God promise to do for our soul?   *restore it*

Our soul includes our mind, emotions and will. Along with spiritual and physical restoration, we also need restoration of our soul. Let's look at some of the ways He restores, refreshes, replenishes and refuels us.

Upload Your Cares

Imagine a marathon runner trying to race wearing a ski jacket, hiking boots and a motorcycle helmet. It would be too big of a burden, and just the weight of the extra clothing alone would wear the runner out! Often in life, we are like that runner. As we run our race, we carry the weight of the world, worries, cares and burdens, which weigh us down. We need to unload. We need to cast our cares on the Lord to get some relief. We need to upload our concerns to the Lord.

1.   Hebrews 12:1

Underline all the things we are to throw off.

> Therefore, since we are surrounded by such a great cloud of
> witnesses, let us throw off everything that hinders and the sin
> that so easily entangles, and let us run with perseverance the
> race marked out for us (NIV).

God has a race for you to run and finish!

How are you to run?

w/ perseverance

What sins and weights could you discard as you keep pace in your race?

Whom do we keep our eyes on in this race?

2.   Psalm 55:22

Underline the phrase "cast your cares on the Lord."

> Cast your cares on the LORD and he will sustain you; he will
> never let the righteous fall (NIV).

Cares are heavy! What does God tell us to do with our cares?

cast them on Him

What worries do you need to hand over to the Lord once and for all?

What does God promise you?

3.   Matthew 11:28-30

Underline verse 30.

Are you tired? Worn out? Burned out on religion? Come to me. Get away with me and you'll recover your life. I'll show you how to take a real rest. Walk with me and work with me — watch how I do it. Learn the unforced rhythms of grace. I won't lay anything heavy or ill-fitting on you. Keep company with me and you'll learn to live freely and lightly (The Message).

If you are tired, worn out, burned out and overloaded, whom should you run to first?

"What a friend we have in Jesus"

What does Jesus want us to do?

watch how He does it

What does Jesus promise you?

In what way is this passage relevant for you?

Know Your Limitations

Sometimes we are our own worst enemy. We don't know how to set boundaries.

We don't say *no.* We create our own stress by not recognizing our God-given limitations.

> NUGGET: It might be good to ask yourself some basic questions. What has God called and gifted you to do? What season of life are you in? Have you recognized the importance of blending your calling and gifts with the season of life you are in? How many plates has God called you to spin? Often, we are stressed in the pace of life because we are putting more pressure on ourselves than God puts on us. Maybe you are the type of person who has a hard time saying no. Maybe you are doing many things that you aren't even called or graced to do. Maybe you are financially overextended in an attempt to keep up with the Joneses. Often, we live beyond our limitations. Real faith recognizes God-ordained boundaries where God's giftings, graces, and callings start and stop. Take some time to think about these things.

1.   Second Corinthians 10:13-16

        Underline the phrase "the field God has assigned to us."

> *We, however, will not boast beyond proper limits, but will confine our boasting to the field God has assigned to us, a field that reaches even to you. We are not going too far in our boasting, as would be the case if we had not come to you, for we did get as far as you with the gospel of Christ. Neither do we go beyond our limits by boasting of work done by others. Our hope is that, as your faith continues to grow, our area of activity among you will greatly expand, so that we can preach the gospel in the regions beyond you. For we do not want to boast about work already done in another man's territory (NIV).*

In this passage, the Holy Spirit through the Apostle Paul explains the importance of knowing your limitations. When we try to do more than God has called us to do, we run the risk of falling into pride, which can lead to overload and burnout. Sure, there may be some people who fit in the "superman" or "superwoman" category and seemingly "do it all," but what has God called you to focus on?

Sometimes we face unnecessary stress and a sense of overload because we are being disobedient in doing more than God desires. Where did Paul say he would spend his ministry efforts?

He determined not to presume authority, rights or gifts that would infringe upon another person's accomplishments or sphere of ministry. How is this passage relevant in your life and staying within your sphere and limitations?

NUGGET: If you are used to operating in God's grace, then it is usually easy to discern when you are operating outside of God's grace. The symptoms of operating outside of God's grace commonly include unusual frustration, dissatisfaction, things just not working, physical symptoms in our bodies, emotional unrest, lack of energy and as someone once put it, "it feels like taking a shower with your socks on!"

2.   John 5:30

Underline the phrases that describe Jesus' submission to God's will.

I am able to do nothing from Myself [independently, of My own accord—but only as I am taught by God and as I get His orders]. Even as I hear, I judge [I decide as I am bidden to decide. As the voice comes to Me, so I give a decision], and My judgment is right (just, righteous), because I do not seek or consult My own will [I have no desire to do what is pleasing to Myself, My own aim, My own purpose] but only the will and pleasure of the Father Who sent Me (AMP).

Jesus, the Master, knew how to stay submitted to God's will. Where did Jesus get His orders?

What was Jesus' focus with His time and energy?

Did Jesus "self-generate" His life and consult His own will?

Who did Jesus want to please?

3.   First Peter 4:10, Romans 12:6

Underline the words "gifts" or "grace."

As each of you has received a gift (a particular spiritual talent, a gracious divine endowment), employ it for one another as [befits] good trustees of God's many-sided grace [faithful stewards of the extremely diverse powers and gifts granted to Christians by unmerited favor] (1 Peter 4:10, AMP).

*Having gifts (faculties, talents, qualities) that differ according
to the <u>grace</u> given us, let us use them (Romans 12:6, AMP).*

In these passages, we are encouraged to use the gifts God has given us. These "grace" gifts are free gifts and abilities the Lord has endowed us with. Living life and serving others is a joy when we operate within our gifting.

What are we to do with our gifts?

Have you identified your God-given gifts? What are they?

Cultivate Your God-Given Friendships

As many friendship experts have said, the relationships in our lives either drain us or energize us. There are high maintenance friends and there are those who pour blessing and refreshment into our lives. Be sure to cultivate the friendships God has given you; they are a gift for refreshing your life.

1.   Romans 15:32

Underline the phrase "be refreshed" and "in your company."

*So that by God's will I may subsequently come to you with joy
(with a happy heart) and be refreshed [by the interval of rest]
in your company (AMP).*

What did Paul say would happen for him and his friends when they were united by God's will?

2.   First Corinthians 16:17-18

Underline the phrase "they've refreshed me."

> *I want you to know how delighted I am to have Stephanas, Fortunatus, and Achaicus here with me. They partially make up for your absence! They've refreshed me by keeping me in touch with you. Be proud that you have people like this among you (The Message).*

How does getting together with godly friends refresh and energize your spirit?

3.   Second Timothy 1:16-18

Underline the words that describe the blessing Onesiphorus was to Paul.

> *The Lord grant mercy to the household of Onesiphorus, for he often refreshed me, and was not ashamed of my chain; but when he arrived in Rome, he sought me out very zealously and found me. The Lord grant to him that he may find mercy from the Lord in that Day — and you know very well how many ways he ministered to me at Ephesus (NKJV).*

Friends who share your love for Christ provide what?

4.   Philemon 7

Underline the phrase "great joy and encouragement" and "refreshed."

Your love has given me great joy and encouragement, because you, brother, have refreshed the hearts of the saints (NIV).

God's love through our friends does what for us?

One of God's greatest blessings is people. Sometimes just talking or praying with a friend does wonders for our stress level. Be sure to appreciate and cultivate the friendships God has placed in your life. You will find relief from much of the stress and overload in your life through these friendships.

Scriptures to Meditate On

"I can do all things through Christ who strengthens me."

Philippians 4:13, NKJV

"Cast your cares on the LORD and he will sustain you;

he will never let the righteous fall."

Psalm 55:22, NIV

Group Discussion

1. Describe the way you cast your cares on the Lord. Is this something you do on a regular basis or do you tend to hold your cares and worries?

2. Describe the season you are in. What assignments, boundaries or limitations does God want you to manage?

3. Describe the energizing friendships God has given you. Who are your "go to" friends in times of crisis, need or joy? In life, some relationships are "draining" and some are "energizing." Talk about how you navigate keeping a balance in your relationships.

CHAPTER 4
BATTERY LIFE

How would you like to run to a tropical island all by yourself, lay in the sun under the beautiful palm trees, read your favorite books and sip fresh-squeezed lemonade? At times, we all want to do this! Unfortunately, we have to snap back into reality because for most of us, escape isn't an option. Stress and overloaded lives are a reality. Other than escaping to a tropical island, is there anything else we can do to eliminate the pressures we face or enlarge the charge required for our lives?

Yes!

At times, we should pull back or cut out things to reduce the demands we face. Yet, in reality, often we can't do anything to eliminate, limit or retreat from our busy lives. So we need another option. Thankfully, we can increase our capacity for dealing with busy lives—we can increase the size of our battery life!

Enlarge the Charge

How many times a day do you look at the amount of battery life you have left on your mobile phone? Do you always carry a charging cable with you? When the "low battery" warning sign flashes on, how does that make you feel? Anxious? Hurried? Do you begin a desperate search for an outlet? These days we can buy larger battery cases for our mobile phones, just to be sure we always have enough battery life to get through the day. Many of us are better at managing the battery life on our mobile phones than we are at managing our own energy. Do you think we should give even more thought and attention to our own personal battery life and our recharging options?

Let's talk about enlarging our charge!

1.   Psalm 4:1

      Underline the word "enlarged."

> *ANSWER ME when I call, O God of my righteousness (uprightness, justice, and right standing with You)! You have freed me when I was hemmed in and <u>enlarged</u> me when I was in distress; have mercy upon me and hear my prayer (AMP).*

When we are in distress and call out to the Lord in prayer, what will He do for us? *free + enlarge*

Enlarge: This means to broaden and is sometimes translated as enlarged, make large, make room, make open wide.[1] When God enlarges, makes large, makes room and makes open wide our hearts, we have the capacity to handle more.

NUGGET: Richard Swenson, author of the excellent book, *Margin: Restoring Emotional, Physical, Financial, and Time Reserves to Overloaded Lives, describes our overloaded lives and our need for margin when he says, "Overload is not having time to finish the book you're reading on stress. Margin is having time to read it twice. Overload is fatigue. Margin is energy. Overload is red ink. Margin is black ink. Overload is hurry. Margin is calm. Overload is anxiety. Overload is the disease of the 90's. Margin is the cure."[2]*

Dr. Swenson provides a <u>prescription against the danger of overloaded lives</u> by focusing on four key areas—emotional energy,

physical energy, time and finances. He shows us how contentment, simplicity, balance and rest provide us with a healthy lifestyle.

In making the case for an enlarged margin, his books says, "As a medical practitioner, Dr. Richard Swenson sees a steady stream of exhausted, hurting people coming into his office. A majority of them are suffering from an uncontrolled societal epidemic: living without margin. Margin is the space that once existed between ourselves and our limits. It's something held in reserve for contingencies or unanticipated situations. As a society, we've forgotten what margin is. In the push for progress, margin has been devoured. So we feel distressed in ill-defined ways. We are besieged by anxiety, stress, and fatigue. Our relationships suffer. We have unexplained aches and pains. The flood of daily events seems beyond our control. We're overloaded. If you yearn for relief from the pain and pressure of overload, take a lifelong dose of Margin under the care of a specialist. The benefits of good health, financial stability, fulfilling relationships, and availability for God's purposes will follow you all your days."3

In the first chapter of Margin, Dr. Swenson describes the scenario of taking a glass of water and adding salt by the teaspoonful. When the salt is stirred into the water, it dissolves. If salt is continually added to the water, eventually the salt will not dissolve. The water is salt saturated and the margin for dissolving salt is over. The only solution is to quit adding salt or to enlarge the cup and then add more water. In our lives, often we cannot stop the salt from coming into our glasses of water, but we can enlarge our container!

The Bible refers to this concept of margin as "enlarged capacity." Let's study several other passages.

2.　　　Second Samuel 22:37

Underline the word "enlarged."

> You <u>enlarged</u> my path under me; so my feet did not slip
> (NKJV).

What will God do to the path we are on?

enlarge it

What does enlarging our path help us with?

so we don't slip

How do you think God enlarges our path?

NUGGET: Have you ever tried to blow up a balloon? The smallest ones are the hardest to inflate. It takes effort and a lot of air pressure to blow up a balloon for the first time. Have you ever noticed that once a balloon is inflated and then deflated, it's quite a bit easier to blow up the next time? This is because the <u>capacity for air was increased the first time it was blown up</u>. The air pressure inside the balloon actually stretched it and enlarged its capacity for future use. In the same manner, God wants to help us keep pace by enlarging our capacity to handle stress and overload. When God begins to enlarge our capacity, it's often tough at first because we feel the pressure. Sometimes it feels like we are going to burst, but usually the Lord allows just enough pressure to enlarge our capacity. Later, when we face other pressures, responsibilities and an increased pace of life, it's amazing how easily our enlarged capacity is able to cope with these things and overcome. It seems that each season of life brings increasing demands. When we are students, young adults or single, there is a certain pace we must keep. As we enter the workforce and take on more responsibility, the pace seems to increase. If we marry and begin a family, the pace picks up again. Many variables factor in over the course of our lives and play a role in determining the stress and overload level we face. For each season that the pace increases, we will likely find God enlarging our capacity and resources to effectively handle the pressures of life.

3.   First Chronicles 4:10

Underline the word "enlarge."

> *And Jabez called on the God of Israel saying, "Oh, that You would bless me indeed, and enlarge my territory, that Your hand would be with me, and that You would keep me from evil, that I may not cause pain!" So God granted him what he requested (NKJV).*

In order to have the influence God had called him to function in, what four things did Jabez need?

What was God's response to Jabez?

Have you prayed this prayer over your own life? Why not do it right now?

4.   Isaiah 54:2-3

Underline the word "enlarge."

> *Enlarge the place of your tent, and let them stretch out the curtains of your dwellings; do not spare; lengthen your cords, and strengthen your stakes. For you shall expand to the right and to the left, and your descendants will inherit the nations, and make the desolate cities inhabited (NKJV).*

God knows all about our lives and future. He helps us prepare for the pace and load we carry.

What did He tell the Israelites to do prior to their increase and growth?

5. Psalm 138:3

Underline the word "large."

> *The moment I called out, you stepped in; you made my life large with strength (The Message).*

The minute we call out to God, He steps in and does what?

6. Isaiah 40:31

Underline the phrase "renew their strength."

> *But those who wait on the LORD shall renew their strength; they shall mount up with wings like eagles, they shall run and not be weary, they shall walk and not faint (NKJV).*

What is the promise to those who wait on the Lord?

God is willing to give us new strength and enlarge our capacity as we call and wait upon Him. God enlarges and charges us with strength, wisdom, knowledge, strategies, energy, ideas, innovation, rest, ability, help and whatever we need.

Scriptures to Meditate On

"But those who wait on the LORD shall renew their strength;

they shall mount up with wings like eagles,

they shall run and not be weary,

they shall walk and not faint."

Isaiah 40:31, NKJV

"Enlarge the place of your tent,

and let them stretch out the curtains of your dwellings;

do not spare; lengthen your cords, and strengthen your stakes.

For you shall expand to the right and to the left"

Isaiah 54:3-4, NKJV

Group Discussion

1. Describe the state of your personal "battery life." Are you staying fully charged or do you sense the "low battery" light coming on often?

2. Describe the "margin" in your life. Do you have any extra margin in any area of your life? Time? Energy? Finances? Mentally? Emotionally? Describe the areas where you need God to enlarge your capacity.

3. Describe the power of waiting on the Lord, and how He enlarges and strengthens you.

----

[1] Biblesoft, Inc. and International Bible Translators, Inc., *New Exhaustive Strong's Numbers and Concordance with Expanded Greek-Hebrew Dictionary.* Copyright © 1994, 2003

[2] Swenson, Richard. *Margin: Restoring Emotional, Physical, Financial, and time Resources to Overloaded Lives.*(Colorado Springs: NavPress, 1995).

[3] iBid,

CHAPTER 5
USER NAME AND PASSWORD

Do you have a place where you keep all your usernames and passwords? How many times have you forgotten your username or password and were unable to access a certain program, app or website? It's frustrating, isn't it?

In God's kingdom, He's given us access to His grace. Our "username" and "password" are appropriated by faith. The big question is this: Are you accessing or frustrating God's grace? It's great to know that God's grace is there to help us, but unfortunately many Christians are not tapping into it. They are not accessing God's grace; they are frustrating it!

Let's take a look at this subject.

Accessing or Frustrating?

1.   Galatians 2:21

        Underline the words "invalidate," "frustrate" and "nullify."

        > [Therefore, I do not treat God's gracious gift as something
        > of minor importance and defeat its very purpose]; I do not
        > set aside and invalidate and frustrate and nullify the grace
        > (unmerited favor) of God (AMP).

        How should we esteem the grace of God?
        as important

God's grace has a purpose and we want to be sure to tap into God's grace and experience its fullest effect in our lives. When we do not esteem, focus on, validate and receive God's grace, we nullify and frustrate its ability to help us.

How do you think we nullify or frustrate God's grace?

become to busy w/ stuff

If you want to avoid frustrating or nullifying God's grace in your life, a good place to start is by simply making this prayerful acknowledgment: *"Father, I believe You have provided grace to help me in everything I face. I need Your grace for the pace I am required to live and I don't want to frustrate or nullify it. I esteem Your grace and I ask You to help me understand and access Your grace by faith. In Jesus' Name. Amen."*

2.   Romans 5:1-2

Underline the phrase "access by faith into this grace."

> *Therefore, since we have been justified through faith, we have peace with God through our Lord Jesus Christ, through whom we have gained access by faith into this grace in which we now stand (NIV).*

What do we have access to through Christ?

when justified through faith

What type of grace are we able to access?

that in w/ch we now stand
→ peace w/ God thru Jesus

How do we access the grace?

thru Jesus

We receive and access God's grace simply by faith. You can't earn it. You can't work for it. You simply access God's grace by faith— believing in your heart and speaking with your mouth. Start believing and speaking God's grace over your life. Access, don't frustrate, the grace for the pace!

What type of grace can we access by faith? Let's take a look.

Access God's Grace to Rule in Life

Romans 5:17

Underline the two things required for reigning in life.

> *how much more will those who receive God's abundant provision of grace and of the gift of righteousness reign in life through the one man, Jesus Christ (NIV).*

What must you receive an abundance of in order to reign in life?

God's grace & righteousness

How would you describe, "reigning in life"?

Living fully in faith

It is God's will that we live in victory. In the face of a busy pace and stress-filled times, God wants us to receive an abundance of His free gift of grace—His supernatural ability—so we can rule in life as kings over anything contrary to His will.

Access God's Grace to Live Life

First Peter 3:7

Underline the words "grace of life."

*problem
w/this.* *

> Husbands, likewise, dwell with them with understanding,
> giving honor to the wife, as to the weaker vessel, and as
> being heirs together of the grace of life, that your prayers may
> not be hindered (NKJV).

Husbands and wives are encouraged to live together in harmony in order to have an effective prayer life. Husbands and wives are to be heirs of what?

the grace of life

How would you describe the "grace of life"?

life w/ God

What would your life look like if you were walking in the "grace of life"?

reflecting God's will for me

Access God's Grace to Strengthen You

Second Corinthians 12:9-10

Underline the results of grace in this passage.

> But He said to me, My grace (My favor and loving-kindness
> and mercy) is enough for you [sufficient against any danger
> and enables you to bear the trouble manfully]; for My strength
> and power are made perfect (fulfilled and completed)
> and show themselves most effective in [your] weakness.

Therefore, I will all the more gladly glory in my weaknesses and infirmities, that the strength and power of Christ (the Messiah) may rest (yes, may pitch a tent over and dwell) upon me! So for the sake of Christ, I am well pleased and take pleasure in infirmities, insults, hardships, persecutions, perplexities and distresses; for when I am weak [in human strength], then am I [truly] strong (able, powerful in divine strength) (AMP).

Is God's grace enough for us?

it should be

What does grace enable us to do?

glory in weakness + infirmities

faith enabled us to see the grace of God

What does grace give us?

strength

xo

How have you experienced this type of grace in your life? Describe it.

Through His grace, God gives us internal, divine strength to stand. When we are weak because of stressors, pressures, persecutions and a fast pace—through His grace we can be strong.

Access God's Grace for Everything You Need

Second Corinthians 9:8

Underline the phrase "all grace."

> *And God is able to make all grace (every favor and earthly blessing) come to you in abundance, so that you may always and under all circumstances and whatever the need be self-sufficient [possessing enough to require no aid or support and furnished in abundance for every good work and charitable donation] (AMP).*

What does God's grace give us?

self-sufficiency, blessings

If you were to receive more of God's grace today, in what areas would you receive it? Ask Him, specifically!

Isn't this encouraging? These things are just the tip of the iceberg concerning the incredible, supernatural help God's grace imparts to us. Let's look at how to pray for more grace!

Pray for Grace

Hebrews 4:16

Underline the phrases "come boldly" and "find grace."

> *Let us therefore come boldly to the throne of grace, that we may obtain mercy and find grace to help in time of need (NKJV).*

God promises to give you grace to help you. The way we access His grace is by coming boldly to His throne of grace.

Why can you come boldly to God's throne?

What does God promise that you can obtain and find?

mercy + grace

Grace in all its forms can be accessed as you go boldly to God's throne in prayer!

Once more, let's pray for grace. *"Father, we are so thankful that because of the blood of Jesus Christ and our union with Him, we can come into Your Presence with boldness. You said we could obtain mercy and find grace to help at Your throne of grace and Father, we thank You for that. Right now, we appropriate Your mercy and grace and we ask You to impart a fresh dose of grace into our lives to help us in every arena. We thank You Lord that right now, we believe we receive a deposit of grace from Your very throne. Thank You. In Jesus' Name. Amen."*

Scriptures to Meditate On

"For the LORD God is a sun and shield;

The LORD will give grace and glory;

No good thing will He withhold

From those who walk uprightly."

Psalm 84:11, NKJV

"how much more will those who receive

God's abundant provision of grace

and of the gift of righteousness

reign in life through the one man, Jesus Christ."

Romans 5:17, NIV

Group Discussion

1. Describe a time when you frustrated God's grace either through ignorance or by not esteeming it.

2. Describe the way you will begin to access God's grace on a more regular basis.

3. Describe some of the specific applications of God's grace you'd like to access more often.

CHAPTER 6
MANAGING YOUR ENERGY

Time management has always been a popular topic for leaders. Energy management is becoming an important subject for high capacity people and top performers. Performance experts are spending a lot of time and charging top dollar to teach leaders how to manage their mental, physical and emotional energy.

God wants us to manage our energy, too. He wants us to use our time wisely. He wants us to get a good return on the use of our spiritual, emotional, mental and physical energy expenditures. He wants us to be good stewards of our lives.

How? By His grace!

God's grace is available to help us manage our energy and organize our time. Time management or more importantly, life management, is an important part of overcoming stress and overload. Many things clutter our lives: schedules, deadlines, commitments, "shoulda, coulda, woulda" thoughts, sin and guilt, a messy home, desk or car, purposeless living—you name it. God wants to help us live an uncluttered life: spirit, soul and body. Let's take a look at the subject of managing our energy and maximizing our lifetime.

Live on Purpose

People waste a lot of time and energy because they lack purpose. Without a purpose it's easy to become apathetic. The writer of Proverbs said, *"He also that is slothful in his work is brother to him that is a great waster" (Proverbs 18:9, KJV)*. When we are lazy and slothful, the pace of life will overtake us. It's important that we live on purpose and fulfill the reason we are alive and on Planet Earth. Let's talk about this.

Ecclesiastes 3:11

Underline the phrase "a divinely implanted sense of a purpose."

> He has made everything beautiful in its time. He also has planted eternity in men's hearts and minds [a divinely implanted sense of a purpose working through the ages which nothing under the sun but God alone can satisfy], yet so that men cannot find out what God has done from the beginning to the end (AMP).

What does this tell us about our purpose?

God has a divinely implanted sense of purpose for you. Isn't that a wonderful thought? You were born for a reason. You are not an accident! God planned for your arrival, whether your parents did or not. He has a divine purpose and plan for you, and it's not His plan or purpose to burn you out with stress, pressure and overload. Have you prayerfully sought the Lord to better identify His purpose for your life or season?

What do you sense God's purpose for your life to be?

Describe the type of energy you are going to need to fulfill your purpose.

NUGGET: Did you know that God's plan for your life is a blessed plan? Often, people have their own ideas and life plans, so they just ask

God to add His blessing to their plans. That's the backwards way to approach life. His blessed plan includes all the grace—energy, know how, favor, strength, wisdom and help you need to fulfill it! Why not seek the Lord for His plan and purpose for your life, knowing that His plan is already blessed? Many people live and die and never once step into their purpose in life. What a tragedy! God's plan and purpose for you will be revealed to your heart as you spend time reading His Word, praying and seeking Him. He's not hiding it from you. Make it your aim to spend some time seeking the Lord and His Word to discover your divinely implanted sense of purpose.

Discipline Yourself

1.   First Corinthians 9:24-27

   Underline the phrase "run in such a way as to get the prize."

   > *Do you not know that in a race all the runners run, but only one gets the prize? Run in such a way as to get the prize. Everyone who competes in the games goes into strict training. They do it to get a crown that will not last; but we do it to get a crown that will last forever. Therefore I do not run like a man running aimlessly; I do not fight like a man beating the air. No, I beat my body and make it my slave so that after I have preached to others, I myself will not be disqualified for the prize (NIV).*

   As we move through life, it's good to know where the finish line is. What goals are you reaching for?

   In what ways could you, or should you, discipline your life—specifically in these areas: personal Bible study, prayer, exercise, diet, giving, time management, mentally, and emotional energy—to win the race?

What type of crown are we running for?

What did the Apostle Paul say he did to himself in order to win and not be disqualified?

gods beat his body + made it his slave

NUGGET: If we want to live a stress-free life, we will have to discipline ourselves. We'll have to make our minds, bodies, and emotions submit to our spirit. Health professionals tell us about the importance of diet and exercise when it comes to releasing the stress in our lives. When it comes to managing our energy, time, relationships, diet, exercise, sleep, time with God, spiritual growth and mental development, it takes discipline. But the payoff is huge—intimacy with God, strength and health in our bodies, peace of mind and favor with God and man. It's worth every bit of determination it takes to live a disciplined life. It goes without saying that if we live the life of a workaholic, alcoholic or foodaholic, we are bound to be stressed and overloaded. If we're addicted or undisciplined, it's likely that our lives will not be what God intended. Let's run, fight the good fight, and keep the faith as we finish the race that is set before us. Let's finish our course with joy!

2.   First Timothy 4:8-9

Underline the phrases "workouts in the gymnasium" and "disciplined life."

Workouts in the gymnasium are useful, but a disciplined life in God is far more so, making you fit both today and forever. You can count on this. Take it to heart (The Message).

When it comes to reducing stress in our lives, fitness training, workouts, diet and rest play an important role. Although we have not focused on this in our study, it is important to consider the fuel and exercise we are giving our bodies and the affect it has on our stress hormones.

As useful as exercise is, what is even more valuable?

Have an Organized Plan

Living a disorganized, unstructured, "fly-by-the-seat-of-the-pants" life will only deplete you of energy and add stress and pressure to an overloaded life. It's true that when we take the time to organize our lives—our work, our homes and our personal lives—we will actually bring a sense of calm, peace and order to our lives.

1.   Proverbs 24:3

        Underline the words "wise planning," "common sense" and "keeping abreast of the facts."

        Any enterprise is built by wise planning, becomes strong through common sense, and profits wonderfully by keeping abreast of the facts (TLB).

        If we want a healthy life, what three things should we pay attention to?

2.   First Corinthians 14:40

Underline the words "decently" and "order."

Let all things be done <u>decently</u> and in <u>order</u> (NKJV).

How should we do things?

In what practical ways could you add order to your life and responsibilities?

NUGGET: One of the best helps for being organized is to begin to think categorically and systematically. For example, I remember when my two boys were around the ages of 5 and 7, and I asked them to clean their bedroom. Their room was a disaster—socks, toys, sports gear, shoes and clothing were all over the place. I moved all the junk to the middle of the room and told them, *"Ok boys, clean your room and I'll check back in about twenty minutes."* They sat down and cried. I realized that this project was overwhelming to their little minds. Where would they begin? I knew that I needed to get them to think categorically and systematically, so I told them we'd take this project in little bites. First, I told them to just search for the socks and put them in a pile, then search for all the little cars and puzzle pieces, and eventually we would whittle the big pile into little piles by organizing things by category.

If the responsibilities, tasks and pace of your life sometimes seem like a big, disorganized, overwhelming pile, take a minute to think about how you could systematically and categorically restructure your life into little piles.

Have you noticed that often when your schedule is organized, your time is managed, and clutter is organized, it clears your mind from stressful and overwhelming thoughts?

What categories could you divide your life into to begin feeling less overwhelmed?

3.   Habakkuk 2:2-3

Underline the phrase "Write the vision."

> *Then the LORD answered me and said: "Write the vision and make it plain on tablets, that he may run who reads it. For the vision is yet for an appointed time; but at the end it will speak, and it will not lie. Though it tarries, wait for it; because it will surely come, it will not tarry (NKJV).*

What should we write down?   *vision*

Do you have a vision or a plan for your life? Family? Career? Ministry? Do you have a plan for this year? This month? This week? Today? Write it down! Write your vision in such a practical way that when you read it, you will be motivated to run with it. Keep it simple. Strategic. Practical.

If you can articulate your vision on paper, it's very likely that this will become your personal roadmap. Often, getting things off our minds and on paper has a way of relieving mental stress and disorganizational overload. Do yourself a favor and write down the things you envision for your life, your year, your month, your week and your day. Also, jot down any plans or strategies the Lord has given you for accomplishing those things.

Maximize Your Time

For every season there is a time!

1.   Psalm 90:12

Underline the phrase "teach us to number our days."

> So <u>teach us to number our days</u> that we may gain a heart of wisdom (NKJV).

God wants us to live life on and with purpose.

How can you number your days?

NUGGET: To calculate a ballpark number of your days, just work this mathematical formula. Take the number of the age you expect and desire to live to be, and subtract your current age from that number. The result will give you a basic number of your days. For example, let's say you are currently 35 years old and you expect to live to be 95 years old. If you subtract 35 from 95, you get 60, right? That tells us that you have around 60 years left.

What is your current age?

To what age do you desire, believe and expect to live?

What is the estimated number of your days?

2.   Psalm 31:15

Underline each word.

My times are in your hands (NIV).

What does it mean to you to know that your times are in God's hands?

3.   Jeremiah 2:8

Underline the phrase "wasted their time on nonsense."

Even their priests cared nothing for the Lord, and their judges
ignored me; their rulers turned against me, and their prophets
worshiped Baal and wasted their time on nonsense (TLB).

This passage tells us that God's ministers were living in an ungodly way. We should not waste our time or energy on things that don't profit others or ourselves.

What can we learn about the use of our time?

What would you consider "nonsense" to be?

4.   Ephesians 5:15-16

Underline the phrase "making the most."

15 Be very careful, then, how you live-not as unwise but as wise, 16 making the most of every opportunity, because the days are evil (NIV).

How should we live?

What does "make the most of every opportunity" mean to you?

NUGGET: Do you have a plan for managing your time and energy? Whether you use a commercial planning system, computer program or create your own, it's amazing how much more effective you can be with your time if you spend some time planning. Also, consider using your time twice. For example, you know you have to eat lunch each day, so why not use your lunch hour to meet with people or to read faith-building or life-enhancing books? By using yearly view and monthly view calendars, checklists and daily planners, you will maximize your time and make the most of every opportunity. Structure your time by scheduling your activities and tasks in blocks. For example: run all your errands at one time, make all your phone conversations during a specific block of time, etc. It's also wise to use your best time, the time when you're most alert, for the most important things. Don't forget about rest and eating properly. I encourage you to be proactive in managing your time, energy and maximizing every moment.

5.   Ecclesiastes 8:5-6

Underline the phrases "a wise man's mind will know" and "right time."

5 ...and a wise man's mind will know both when and what to do. 6 For every purpose and matter has its [right] time and judgment (AMP).

What does a wise man know?

What does every purpose and matter have?

There is grace for the pace! As we learn to live on purpose, to live with an organized plan and to maximize our time, we will find that order brings a great sense of energy, stability and freedom from stress to our lives.

Scriptures to Meditate On

"To every thing there is a season,

and a time to every purpose under the heaven"

Ecclesiastes 3:1, KJV

"a wise man's mind will know both when and what to do.

For every purpose and matter has its [right] time and judgment"

Ecclesiastes 8:5-6, AMP

Group Discussion

1. Describe what you understand about God's purpose for your life. Share any verses of Scripture the Lord has given you about your purpose.

2. Describe the areas of your life that need more discipline, vision and planning.

3. Describe your plan for managing your time and energy and numbering your days.

About the Author
Beth Jones

Beth Jones and her husband Jeff are the founders and senior pastors of Valley Family Church in Kalamazoo, Michigan, planted in 1991 and named by Outreach magazine as one of the fastest growing churches in America in 2009 and 2010. They also lead Jeff and Beth Jones Ministries, an organization dedicated to helping people *get the basics*. Beth and Jeff have four children who are all involved in leadership and ministry.

Beth grew up in Lansing, Michigan, and was raised as a Catholic. At the end of her freshman year in college, she came into a personal relationship with Christ through the testimony of her roommate. It was there, at age 19, that she realized God's plan for her to preach and teach the gospel through writing and speaking. She has been following that call ever since.

Beth is the author of 20 books, including the popular *Getting a Grip on the Basics* series, which is being used by thousands of churches in America and has been translated into over a dozen foreign languages and used around the world. She also writes *The Basics Daily Devo*, a free daily edevotional for thousands of subscribers.

The heart of Beth's message is simple: *"I exist to help people get the basics!"* Through her practical, down-to-earth teaching, she inspires people to enjoy an authentic relationship with Jesus, to take Him at His Word, and to reach their greatest God-given potential!

Beth attended Boston University in Boston, Massachusetts and received her ministry training at Rhema Bible Training Center in Tulsa, Oklahoma.

For more spiritual growth resources or to connect with Beth, please visit:

www.valleyfamilychurch.org

www.jeffandbethjones.com

www.facebook.com/jeffandbethjones

www.twitter.com/bethjones

www.instagram.com/bethjone

PRAYER OF SALVATION

God loves you—no matter who you are, no matter what your past. God loves you so much that He gave His one and only begotten Son for you. The Bible tells us that "...whoever believes in Him shall not perish but have eternal life" (John 3:16 NIV). Jesus laid down His life and rose again so that we could spend eternity with Him in heaven and experience His absolute best on earth. If you would like to receive Jesus into your life, say the following prayer out loud and mean it from your heart.

Heavenly Father, I come to You admitting that I am a sinner. Right now, I choose to turn away from sin, and I ask You to cleanse me of all unrighteousness. I believe that Your Son, Jesus, died on the cross to take away my sins. I also believe that He rose again from the dead so that I might be forgiven of my sins and made righteous through faith in Him. I call upon the name of Jesus Christ to be the Savior and Lord of my life. Jesus, I choose to follow You and ask that You fill me with the power of the Holy Spirit. I declare that right now I am a child of God. I am free from sin and full of the righteousness of God. I am saved in Jesus' name. Amen.

If you prayed this prayer to receive Jesus Christ as your Savior for the first time, please contact us on the Web at **www.harrisonhouse.com** to receive a free book.

Or you may write to us at

Harrison House • P.O. Box 35035 • Tulsa, Oklahoma 74153

Mary Ellen   Karen C
Sue   Donnette
Sarah   Nancy
Julie   Jean
Jo Ellen   Pam
Marge   me

The Harrison House Vision

Proclaiming the truth and the power

Of the Gospel of Jesus Christ

With excellence;

Challenging Christians to

Live victoriously,

Grow spiritually,

Know God intimately.

743 - WTTW

Equador